Prick Thorns

Life & Family

MAME YAA

ISBN 978-1-95081-807-5 (paperback)

Copyright © 2019 by Mame Yaa

All rights reserved. No part of this publication may be reproduced, distributed, or transmitted in any form or by any means, including photocopying, recording, or other electronic or mechanical methods without the prior written permission of the publisher. For permission requests, solicit the publisher via the address below.

Rushmore Press LLC
1 888 733 9607
www.rushmorepress.com

Scripture quotations marked KJV are from the Holy Bible, King James Version (Authorized Version). First published in 1611. Quoted from the KJV Classic Reference Bible, Copyright © 1983 by Zondervan Corporation.

Scripture quotations marked NIV are taken from the Holy Bible, New International Version®. Copyright © 1973, 1978, 1984 by International Bible Society. Used by permission of Zondervan. All rights reserved. [Biblica]

Contents

Chapter 1: My Woman,
My Husband And
Our Relationship 5

Chapter 2: Team Time Family 13

Chapter 3: Family Love 22

Chapter 4: Healthy Communication 30

Chapter 5: Who Is Our Mentor And
Head In The Family? 40

Chapter 6: Negative Power 51

Chapter 7: Being Unsatisfied 60

One

MY WOMAN, MY HUSBAND AND OUR RELATIONSHIP

This is my belief that a relationship is a strong connection that we build and have with somebody through blood, marriage, adoption, friendship, etc. and the way we behave towards each other would either maintain that bond or not . To me a relationship is a process that does not have a definite end. The stronger it is built the better it gets; the weaker it is built the more problematic it becomes. It is a form of partnership where both parties agreed intentionally or unintentionally to build a future together. These partners do not know their end from their beginning so they endure trials and uncertainties to maintain that unknown future. There are some who along the line give up, others continue till they succeed. This is why to me it is a long journey and it takes courage to take it.

God is the initiator of relationships and He orders us to respect it in any kind of form that is perfect in his sight. In my opinion relationship starts with the basic of two and then grow to become more. The verses below help identify kinds of relationship that we have.

1. **1 Timothy 5:8 But if anyone does not provide for his relatives, and especially for members of**

his household, he has denied the faith and is worse than an unbeliever.

2. **Exodus 20:12** "Honor your father and your mother, that your days may be long in the land that the LORD your God is giving you.

3. **Genesis 2:24** Therefore a man shall leave his father and his mother and hold fast to his wife, and they shall become one flesh.

4. **Ephesians 6:1-4** Children, obey your parents in the Lord, for this is right. "Honor your father and mother" (this is the first commandment with a promise), "that it may go well with you and that you may live long in the land." Fathers, do not provoke your children to anger, but bring

them up in the discipline and instruction of the Lord.
5. **1 Peter 2:18** Servants, be subject to your masters with all respect, not only to the good and gentle but also to the unjust
6. **Colossians 4:1** Masters, treat your slaves justly and fairly, knowing that you also have a Master in heaven
7. **Proverbs 18:24** "One who has unreliable friends soon comes to ruin, but there is a friend who sticks closer than a brother
8. **Proverbs 17:17** "A friend loves at all times, and a brother is born for adversity.

If having and building a relationship was not good God will not create two people in the first place. You can choose not to have a relationship with anyone but you will be lonely and unhealthy. A house that is not occupied by anybody breaks easily. We usually encounter problems through our relationships yet those problems builds us and make us strong to withstand uncertainties in our lives.

Relationship is not a one way road; but it is about give and take

- When you love your wife and respect her; she becomes humble to you and give you respect
- When you love your children and assume your responsibilities for them they honor and respect you
- When you consider and respect your workers; they give you their loyalty

These are but a few to mention. You reap what you sow.

Relationship is also about sharing: we share our

- ❖ Feelings- love, care, emotions, warmth etc.

- ❖ Time and space for positive reactions and sometimes for the negative which is not a good idea.
- ❖ Thoughts- through word and actions
- ❖ Finances- for a goal etc.

This is where the connection starts getting stronger and grow. Why because the other party now has a piece of you with him/her and most of the time it is difficult to let go what comfort us. So we try to work hard to keep it and cherish it. So in this wise the relationship now has a solid beginning.

Problems arises throughout this journey and could be a thorn on our side if not taken care of immediately.

A thorn is something that wounds, annoy or cause discomfort and a thorn in one's side or flesh is a source of continual irritation or suffering. Thorns are usually found on plants and we all know that plants have life in them and so does the thorn. As the plant grows so does the thorn as the plant survives so does the thorn but when the plant dies the thorn is still able to prick. A thorn is very dangerous because it does not spare anybody or a thing it comes in contact with, it only leaves a painful scar and memory of it on the person. Therefore if one has a thorn in one's side it needs to be dealt with as soon as possible. Now the prick of the thorn is the sharp pointed edge of the thorn which penetrates or puncture through the skin without mercy leaving a stingy pain on the body. Therefor along this family journey we need to watch out for these hidden problems and uproot them before we get hurt by them.

Two

TEAM TIME FAMILY

Relationship is a plural word- thus you become a team in the family and you no longer rely on yourself anymore but on the team to be successful. In so doing, decision making, difficult times and the support each one need, now becomes the team's responsibility is not only on you. So you bear the weight but not all the weight since it is teamwork.

In this team of family members, each of you have a part to play in providing good services towards one another. Do not judge one another because of a weakness they showed in the process but be considerate towards each other so that the stronger one will lift the weaker to also be strong and this will produce harmony in the home. In time of difficulties, there are good counsels and profitable advices that lift the spirits of the team and bring more advantages than disadvantages.

We know that if the house or family members are not harmonious each one will pursue their own selfish agendas and interests. These individuals talk far more about themselves than others wanting the other to see all their problems and gains. They only love you when you give an ear to them. They are so self-centered. They usually eat with you, chitchat with you and even flatter you but they do not help you for your own good.

Such members they try to be happy when they see you being happy or even celebrate with you on your best occasions but they disappear or even laugh behind your back when you fall.

But a family with a good team based environment, there is the demand to make responsible decisions, and interact at a much different level with the team; this promotes excellent interpersonal skills. They show interest in the profit of the team than seek their own pleasure. The success of the team is the focus for them so in difficult times they do not leave but rather grow closer to the others. They understand sacrifice and don't care if they have to do it themselves to see another prosper. Another person's joy is their own joy. They seek peace with others than their own selfish gain over others. They understand true love.

Advantages of a Team Family-

- ❖ Their counsel is from the heart- you will find sincerity, honesty, and affection in their advice or directions.
- ❖ Their counsel brings comfort and friendliness
- ❖ Their counsel stirs the spirit with confidence, hope and joy
- ❖ In the end of it there is always thanksgiving on the lips of the team
- ❖ They are not envious of each other but share both sorrow and joy
- ❖ They don't flatter but speak truthfully
- ❖ They protect each other

- ❖ They give their all for the common goal than to take or dwell on what others have achieved.
- ❖ They do not produce or live in fear but they love and depend on each other treating the other with respect.
- ❖ They rebuke and warn the other of danger instead of hiding the truth behind a smile.

Ecclesiastes 4:9-12 Two *are* better than one; because they have a good reward for their toil. 10 For if they fall, the one will lift up his fellow: but woe to him *that is* alone when he falleth; for *he hath* not another to help him up. 11 Again, if two lie together, then they have heat: but how …

When some members in the family or team don't do their part, it affects the rest of the family but when they do, this brings about togetherness which in turn builds a good family relationship.

I. **Where members show ingratitude:**

2 Timothy 3:2

For people will be lovers of self, lovers of money, proud, arrogant, abusive, disobedient to their parents, ungrateful, unholy.

Philippians 4:6-8

[6] do not be anxious about anything, but in everything by prayer and supplication with thanksgiving let your requests be made known to God.[7] and the peace of God, which surpasses all understanding, will guard your hearts and your minds in Christ Jesus.

⁸ Finally, brothers, whatever is true, whatever is honorable, whatever is just, whatever is pure, whatever is lovely, whatever is commendable, if there is any excellence, if there is anything worthy of praise, think about these things.

Ingratitude is one of the thorns that pricks us as much without us noticing it. As people, we can be self-absorbed and self-centered so much that we tend to forget who our creator is and the need of our neighbors. Yet we strife hard to chase after money and other desires which intend leaves us with pride. Most of the time we do not even care about how others feel but in the end we tend to abuse them for our gain.

1 Samuel 25:20

Now David had said, "Surely in vain I have guarded all that this man has in the

wilderness, so that nothing was missed of all that belonged to him; and he has returned me evil for good.

Romans 1:20

For even though they knew God, they did not honor Him as God or give thanks, but they became futile in their speculations, and their foolish heart was darkened.

Now being ungrateful and unholy is one of the things that God detests therefore in everything lets us give thanks to God in our daily lives let us show humility, be just in our actions, and honorable in our doings. And let's be generous and appreciate God and our neighbors. We toil so much to achieve our goals and when by the Grace of God we get what we need we still compare ourselves to others and their wealth. If only we would be content and show thanks to God for his daily provision in our lives would he continue to bless us because he has said in James 4:10 that we should humble ourselves and he will lift us up.

Three

FAMILY LOVE

If there is no love in the family or among the team, the family would be dysfunctional. The relationship will now become a burden on everyone and this can affect the state of mind among the members. There is no anticipation to see the other. And nobody assumes responsibility for the other.

- ❖ One person has more power or control over others and demands

that the others do what he or she says or wants.
- ❖ There are manipulations of emotions in trying to get the others to respond by the creation of feelings of guilt, pity or jealousy.
- ❖ The others always take and not contribute anything
- ❖ There are no clear cut expectations so each member do not even know what they are fighting for.

Having team love does not mean that there would be no argument at all, but how the team grow from and accept mistakes will set the platform for peace where love can sail through easily. But where members want to compete against each other the platform created instead of peace become war. The interactions with others become surface-level issues with hidden agendas behind smiles. Where the love dominates- the members feel safe around each other, nobody cares about impressing the other, but work needs to be done here thus creating friendship and maintaining it to the point where children can confide in the parents, wife can confide in Husband and husband likewise. This maintain and influence good health because the members have no qualms with each other. There is also trust amongst members and this reduces stress and improve mental health. Family members have courage to face each other every day with much energy. Why?

- Members feel secured
- Members feel they are being treated fairly
- Members feel involved and so they easily cooperate

- Members are allowed to feel responsible for actions
- Members are allowed to grow with much support
- Members are not looked down upon
- Members always have a place to call home that they can go back to anytime.

i. **Where there is lack of enjoyment among members:**

Ecclesiastes 4:8

There was a man all alone; he had neither son nor brother. There was no end to his toil, yet his eyes were not content with his wealth. "For whom am I toiling," he asked, "and why am I depriving myself of enjoyment?" This too is meaningless-- a miserable business!

Ecclesiastes 5:10

Whoever loves money never has enough; whoever loves wealth is never satisfied with their income. This too is meaningless.

There is lack of enjoyment in our lives because we first of all take God out of the equation and are never satisfied with what we have. One would ask, but I have bills to pay so shouldn't I work for the money? Or another would say, but I need money for this and that.

My answer is yes we all need money to survive and is essential in our daily lives; after all God has said a hand that does not work should not eat. <For even when we were with you, we would give you this command: If anyone is not willing to work, let him not eat. **2 Thessalonians 3:10**>

Deuteronomy 8:18

But remember the LORD your God, for it is he who gives you the ability to produce wealth, and so confirms his covenant, which he swore to your ancestors, as it is today.

What I want to say is that we have developed a lifestyle of doing anything to get the money and the desires of our heart; deceiving others for it, bullying others for it and sometimes using dubious means to get it. At certain times, we may be doing the right things but we go all out at it and never give ourselves a break or even have time for our family members. We are always stressed out over what we have and see more of our problems than the solutions and so we strive hard to look for other means to get it.

So my question is, why and who are really working so hard for?

Some will say I am doing this for my child; but have you ever paused to look back or check to see if that is what your child really needs. Sometimes our family need a little attention from us and they tell us in so many indirect ways to take a break and relax. But look at yourself, you will crush everything in your way to lay your hands on that money or that thing you are seriously pursuing whether good or bad without even spending a penny to your satisfaction and leaving your family in the miserable state which the money can't even repair.

We all have desires and things we want to achieve; list every one of your priorities down and you would realize that only one is very important and the rest are just your wants and not your needs. God said **<Commit thy works unto the LORD, and thy thoughts shall be established. Proverbs 16:3>**

Commit everything you do to the LORD. Trust him, and he will help you. Psalm 37:5

Trust in the LORD with all your heart and lean not on your own understanding; Proverbs 3:5

So what are you going to do? Your way or God's way which leads to life and good rest and of course sound mind and good health. And as well with no regrets.

Four

HEALTHY COMMUNICATION

This is one of the important areas in a relationship that set as a pillar and when a crack comes through and it is not fixed immediately can get the whole relationship to collapse. Sometimes members have no idea where the crack was or how the crack came about in the first place because they forget that they have been neglecting unsolved issues, and these issues or problems have intensified to this point. If only members would agree that each individual in the family have needs and wants and that if each could identify them; then it would be easy to place value for each other where necessary.

In a healthy communication platform, one is allowed to:

- Speak up their mind defensively but not offensively- offending people unnecessarily can be a dangerous thread to walk upon. Just because you are speaking your mind shouldn't make you disrespect the other or look down on them.
- To respect members' privacies- not everyone would want to share every information when it comes to sensitive matters and to them they need us to respect that

until they are ready to talk about them and so we need to allow them their space.

- Exercise right control over children but not to obsessed or become possessive of them and also between husband and wife there is no need for power and control but to exercise respect and love. This makes the members feel they are part of the family otherwise there would always be that feeling of boss and a worker or a master and slave. Nobody wants that in their own home.

Education starts from the home therefore being able to communicate through teaching the children the value of teamwork encourages our relationship with them. We have to be models and practice what we teach them because they are watching and they pick what they see not what they hear.

Children are vulnerable and their curiosity very high so they think they can do anything and everything that seem right to them and usually they are all wrong so as a parent what do you do? You knowing that the path is not right, all you can do is to communicate. But how well you do it is a skill and a process that both of you must take and go through. The child needs to know that he or she is not alone and that there is another choice they can make. Sometimes when our children make mistakes we as parents tend to single them out and make them feel naked and shy and also so guilty that they feel that is it; nobody cares for them. They now tend to arrogance and pride to get back at you. But in their mess if we could pick them up and hold them in our arms with a smile on our face and talk to them about the other choice it could have made a lot of difference than to single them out in your anger and telling them about their faults without offering solutions and telling them to figure the right path on their own. That really is a huge task. This is where unnecessary stuff and people begin to fill your place in their minds because you have neglected your duty to be the one who fill their minds with right choices. Have fun with your own kids and family so that they do not feel left out but be confident wherever they find themselves. Some men and women are so stingy when it comes to having fun with their children then, how do you expect them to be happy and know about social life. Yet when they grow up and they distant themselves from you, you think they are mean but that is what you taught them and that is what they learnt.

Let us create a happy environment for our own household so that we can enjoy the fruits we bear and have no regrets. Husbands don't talk to your wives as you would to a kid and don't talk to your kids as you would to your wife and wives vice versa. This leads to creating a balanced home where respect is a value.

i. **Where the family takes useless Endeavors:**

Ecclesiastes 1:14
I have seen all the things that are done under the sun; all of them are meaningless, a chasing after the wind.

Sometimes we strive so hard to achieve a goal that we have set so much that we begin to forget the meaning and reason why we even started the goal in the first place. Imagine a husband and wife working so hard to build a house and live comfortably, they work so much towards achieving that goal that they neglect their marriage and allow their marriage to crumble. So what was the use of getting the comfortable house if you would lose your marriage in the end? Whatever God is not in is vain.

We have to be able to discern between good and bad times and enquire from God what we should do before we make steps into the unknown.

Isaiah 44:17-20

[17] And the rest of it he makes into a god, his idol, and falls down to it and worships it. He prays to it and says, "Deliver me, for you are my god!"

¹⁸ They know not, nor do they discern, for he has shut their eyes, so that they cannot see, and their hearts, so that they cannot understand. ¹⁹ No one considers, nor is there knowledge or discernment to say, "Half of it I burned in the fire; I also baked bread on its coals; I roasted meat and have eaten. And shall I make the rest of it an abomination? Shall I fall down before a block of wood?" ²⁰ He feeds on ashes; a deluded heart has led him astray, and he cannot deliver himself or say, "Is there not a lie in my right hand?"

I was once watching a movie and in it some men had carved a wooden god and were carrying it along in the ship they were in. but when there was a shipwreck, the wooden god fell in the water and could not save them even though they prayed to it.

I thought; what are these people doing, don't they know that the god couldn't save itself nonetheless save them as well.

It brought my mind to how we have created certain idol names and material idols for ourselves, some even want others to worship them so much that without those things they are nothing and when they are being attacked by the very things or names they have created for themselves and realize these things can't save them, they begin to crumble and want to die.

But remember in Exodus 20:2-3 the Lord our God said:

1. **You shall have no other gods before me.**
2. **You shall not make idols.**

3. You shall not take the name of the LORD your God in vain.

And this was also confirmed in Deuteronomy 5:6-11

Five

WHO IS OUR MENTOR AND HEAD IN THE FAMILY?

We all know the father or husband is the head of the family, yet above him is Christ. So he cannot do anything without an agreement with Christ or else it will come to naught. The family depends on the husband and the husband depends on God which brings all the family's dependency on God. A husband who commits his life to depend on God is able to take responsibility for his family. Then he is able to love and give good directions to members. He becomes a pillar the family looks up to and with his directions the family is able to work towards a common goal.

In a family where selfish gains are what the leads desire; we identify selfishness, deception and pride in them. They are like rebels who fights against anything that is good. These leads whether the man or the woman, creates a path for others to walk on; one that does not bring a good end.

In today's world- many selfish men and women work extremely hard using any means to acquire inheritance for themselves and their children and also for power and positions disregarding the consequences and the aftermath of their actions. Sometimes based on the level of achievements, family background and education, their influence becomes great and to them that is their power, and instead of knowing these things are foolish and vain they would rather build their confidence around it and use it to lead people astray. These people are really never happy in life because there is always a constant grief at the corner that always lurks at them.

- Pride- our own pride makes us look down on our husbands and children, families and others. We may earn more money or have high level of education or hold high positions than others but this does not give us the right to look down and disgrace others. These titles are to help us bring and direct others towards the right and knowledgeable path.

Yet a prideful woman makes her husband feel his worth is less and lacks authority of the home. Wife; remember, when you gain the upper hand and steps into your husband's shoes there is no place for him again so he steps aside and watch you stress yourself over everything. Wife, as you complain there is nothing he can do because you have not given his position back to him yet. Remember when men don't find themselves useful in the house they will look elsewhere. Sometimes they indulge themselves with different women for sex, or they get addicted to drinking or smoking or any useless thing that fill the gap that has been created. You will lose your husband this way-

let down your pride and take your proper position in the home.
- **In the case where one or some members are doing evil:**

The bible says do not conform to the things of this world but be transformed by the renewing of your mind...

What do you think about all the time and what do you see in your mind's eye? In your imaginations do you find God there, do you seek to please him in repentance or think the whole world is against you? Who and what do you fight with all the time? I tell you because there is no love in you, for God is love and he tells us to love Him with all our heart, soul, and strength and also to love our neighbors as ourselves.

As human as we are we enjoy doing bad things to ourselves and to others without our conscience pricking us. To us we are Christians and think we are doing what God wants us to do but, we ignore the little things we do to offend each other and think that is ok. If it was ok why do you feel pain and insecure in your heart when you see your neighbor. Why do you not want to talk to such a person?

1 Peter 4:15 "But let none of you suffer as a murderer or a thief or an evildoer or as a meddler."

Luke 13:27 "But he will reply, 'I don't know you or where you come from. Away from me, all you evildoers!'

Psalm 34:16 "The face of the LORD is against evildoers, to cut off the memory of them from the earth."

Proverbs 17:4 "An evildoer listens to wicked lips; a liar pays attention to a destructive tongue."

This is another thorn that pricks us most of the time thus we always think we are better than others. Sometimes for the small material things we possess we assume we are high and mighty and tries to trample on others; but let me ask you; what do you have that it was not given to you by God?

We tend to gossip about others so intensely we forget about our own mistakes. Slandering their name and reputation as well as destroying their character. (Proverbs 6:16-19).

So who said that the one who said it, is only at fault, the one who listened and spread the rumor is also wicked because in the end someone can die both physically and spiritually. Therefore let us rebuke such people when they approach us. The Lord says resist the devil and he shall flee.

We do evil to ourselves and think we are on top of the world

- Smoking all kinds of stuff into our bodies in the end all we can get is sickness
- Drinking alcohol and all manner of vain drinks making us loose ourselves and sanity there is shame and disgrace lurking at you
- Having illicit sexual affairs when we are supposed to have one wife or husbands stroke and other heavy sickness awaits you.

Have you forgotten that we are the temple of God and that he does not dwell in the houses that man has made except what HE God has made? That is why HE made us into his own image and after his likeness so stop destroying yourself and seek after God's kingdom and his righteousness.

1 Peter 4:3 For you have spent enough time in the past doing what pagans choose to do—living in debauchery, lust, drunkenness, orgies, carousing and detestable idolatry

Ephesians 5:18 do not get drunk on wine, which leads to debauchery. Instead, be filled with the Spirit,

Proverbs 31:4-5 It is not for kings, Lemuel— it is not for kings to drink wine, not for rulers to crave beer, 5 lest they drink and forget what has been decreed, and deprive all the oppressed of their rights.

1 Corinthians 10:23 "I have the right to do anything, you say–but not everything is

beneficial. I have the right to do anything–but not everything is constructive."

Ephesians 4:22 "You were taught, with regard to your former way of life, to put off your old self, which is being corrupted by its deceitful desires."

1 Corinthians 6:19

"What? Know ye not that your body
is the temple of the Holy Ghost
which is in you, which ye have of
God, and ye are not your own?"

1 Corinthians 3:17 - If any man defile the temple of God, him shall God destroy; for the temple of God is holy, which [temple] ye are.

1 Peter 5:8 - Be sober, be vigilant; because your adversary the devil, as

a roaring lion, walketh about, seeking whom he may devour:

Romans 6:16 New International Version (NIV)

¹⁶ Don't you know that when you offer yourselves to someone as obedient slaves, you are slaves of the one you obey—whether you are slaves to sin, which leads to death, or to obedience, which leads to righteousness?

Six

NEGATIVE POWER

There are certain women and some men as well who emerges as power house behind their husbands or to the families that lead large corporations or head institutions or even head countries etc. their influence are intense to the point of manipulating their husbands, wives and children and sometimes other leaders involved, by encouraging certain rituals and unnecessary killings all to cover up for one wrong thing they did. If only they could have owned up to their wrongs these would have stopped. They challenge authorities and control them to their favor disregarding consequences. They use scare tactics to frighten many into silence. Sometimes they pay others to use fear, guilt, intimidation, blaming, and manipulation to control others for their gain. You are a really bad person. The idea of being the boss has filled their head and so they crave for power and more power and always wants to be in charge even in their husbands' presence. Seeing people do what they say sort of entice them and so they crave more and more power doing crazy stuff.

- Negative outlook- negative women and men are toxic and bad for the health of the people around them. Their negativity would be eventually transferred to others because they spend most time with them. A negative woman or man does not know how to compromise when things don't go well with him or her; the blame is always on somebody else. They cannot accept the flaws of others they easily get offended by them. They can't stand to be skipped over with an opportunity they thought they really deserved. Based on their attitude they would use their influence to bring the other down regardless of whether they qualified or not. Selfishness seems to be the food they eat every day. Others take responsibility for their actions because unknowingly, their

thoughts, behaviors, and feelings have been influenced or bought.
- There is no love in them –

1 Corinthians 13:4-7 English Standard Version (ESV)

⁴ Love is patient and kind; love does not envy or boast; it is not arrogant ⁵ or rude. It does not insist on its own way; it is not irritable or resentful;[a] ⁶ it does not rejoice at wrongdoing, but rejoices with the truth. ⁷ Love bears all things, believes all things, hopes all things, and endures all things.

I. Patience is one of the fruit of the spirit but because they have none they cannot exercise it. There is no patience in them and for others. They do wrong but cannot tolerate others faults. Because of this it is difficult for

them to stay calm all the time and so mentally they are not healthy.
II. they envy what others have and boasts in what they have
III. If they have the upper hand they really are arrogant thinking they are better than others.
IV. they usually insist on what they want with less consideration for others
V. Every good thing which happens to another irritates them; they should have been the ones instead, they think; and so they hide resentment in their hearts toward others.
VI. They rejoice to see others hurt sometimes they are the one who hurt them.

Psalm 140:12 English Standard Version (ESV)

I know that the LORD will maintain the cause of the afflicted, and will execute justice for the needy.

Repent for the Lord will execute justice for those that you oppress. Besides those that you bully, they really do not respect you it is just that they have not voiced out yet on the day you fall none of them will help in fact, they will really help you fall very fast.

Deuteronomy 24:14

"You shall not oppress a hired servant who is poor and needy, whether he is one of your countrymen or one of your aliens who is in your land in your towns.

Exodus 22:22

"You shall not afflict any widow or orphan.

Proverbs 22:22

Do not rob the poor because he is poor, or crush the afflicted at the gate

Jeremiah 22:17

"But your eyes and your heart Are intent only upon your own dishonest gain, and on shedding innocent blood and on practicing oppression and extortion."

Psalm 73:8

They mock and wickedly speak of oppression; they speak from on high.

Psalm 119:134

Redeem me from the oppression of man, that I may keep your precepts.

Vain desires –

- compliments
  These people like to be complimented every day and they live their life on praises. They don't do well on criticism and so they easily crumble when this happens unexpectedly.

- For most of these women and men their titles seem to be more important to them than their families because they feel respected through it.

- The platform of being around other people with influence eat into their head so much it becomes dangerous for them when they can't be at par with them.

- Domineering – they don't like to listen to any instructions or advise especially if the advice is coming from one they think is beneath their status. They retaliate when they are criticized- if they are the ones above; they would make you lose your opportunity and if they are beneath they destroy what you love.

Seven

BEING UNSATISFIED

There are those who build their house through unjust means setting their nest on high to escape the clutches of ruin. These people plot to ruin others for their gain they do not mind to steal from whoever they work for to gain material things and acquire so much assets to make people bow down to them. They do not show respect or fear the Lord and his punishment because they assume the Lord is far away and can't see them yet they are afraid to be caught by the law so they do everything to cover up their wrong doings. So God has also blinded them so that they wallow in their sin for the day of shame and judgment.

Isaiah 29:8

It will be as when a hungry man dreams-- And behold, he is eating; But when he awakens, his hunger is not satisfied, Or as when a thirsty man dreams-- And behold, he is drinking, But when he awakens, behold, he is faint And his thirst is not quenched. Thus the multitude of all the nations will be who wage war against Mount Zion.

Ecclesiastes 6:7

All a man's labor is for his mouth and yet the appetite is not satisfied.

Isaiah 55:2

"Why do you spend money for what is not bread, and your wages for what does not satisfy? Listen carefully to me, and eat what is good, and delight yourself in abundance.

Why are we not satisfied with what we have and not show contentment with what we have been blessed with? Most of the time it is because of our pride and the "we want more syndrome"; I haven't achieved enough yet, we say. Being unsatisfied steers us to incorrectly influence our lives and keep us in bondage. We want to be rewarded but we will not go the extra mile. We complain about everything we do yet we want to be praised and respected. We compare ourselves with others too much that we skip the opportunity to be content and instead develop bitterness in our hearts. If we cannot be happy and praise God with what we have, but keep wanting to have what the other person have then our path is leading to greed so how can God bless us. The Bible said if you are faithful in the little then you can be faithful in the much he would give.

Matthew 25:23

His master said to him, 'Well done, good and faithful servant. You have been faithful over a little; I will set you over much. Enter into the joy of your master.'

Colossians 3:23-24

Whatever you do, work at it with all your heart, as working for the Lord, not for human masters, since you know that you will receive an inheritance from the

Lord as a reward. It is the Lord Christ you are serving.

Why race through life when you can do better today. Even if you did not get what you need or want, did you do something you will regret forever?

- Did you hurt somebody?
- Did somebody hurt you and what did you do or think?
- Did you boast about something or were you humble to let others see God.

James 4:10 NIV

Humble yourselves before the Lord, and he will lift you up.

Amos 5:14 NIV

Seek good, not evil, that you may live. Then the Lord God Almighty will be with you, just as you say he is.

Proverbs 11:18

A wicked person earns deceptive wages, but the one who sows righteousness reaps a sure reward.

www.ingramcontent.com/pod-product-compliance
Lightning Source LLC
Chambersburg PA
CBHW030133100526
44591CB00009B/639